What's special to me

Religious Articles
Objects used in worship

Anita Ganeri

WAYLAND

Contents

All Wayland books encourage children to read and help them improve their literacy.

✔ The contents page, page numbers, headings and index help to locate a particular piece of information.

✔ The glossary reinforces alphabetic knowledge and extends vocabulary.

✔ The books to read section suggests other books dealing with the same subject.

Special Things

Do you have a favourite item? It might be a toy, a badge or a piece of clothing. What makes it so special to you?

Religions have many things that have a special meaning. They are used as part of worship to remind people about their beliefs.

Hindu Worship

When Hindus worship, they make offerings to a god or goddess. This god or goddess is shown by images or pictures and is a way of **showing** God. Here is the god **Krishna**. He is an important god for many Hindus.

Some Hindus offer garlands of flowers, fruit and sweets to the gods when they worship. They believe the gods give them their blessing in return. Some Hindus buy offerings from a market stall like this one.

When Hindus worship at a **mandir**, a red mark, called a tilak, is placed on the worshipper's forehead by a priest. This shows that he or she has been blessed by the gods.

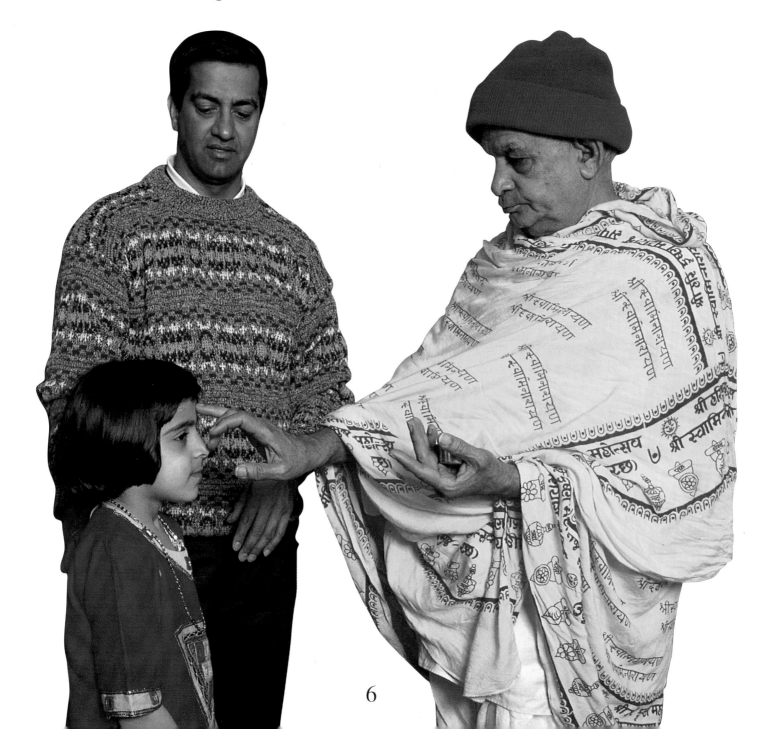

As part of worship Hindus light small
lamps called **divas**. They hold their hands
over the flames and touch their heads and
faces to feel the gods' blessing. Hindus can
also worship the gods at home.

Jewish Articles of Prayer

Some Jewish boys and men wear special religious clothes as part of worship. The cap is called a kippah and shows respect for God. The prayer shawl is called a tallit. It reminds the wearer to obey God's laws.

Two small leather boxes called tefillin are
also worn for worship. Inside the boxes are
writings from the **Torah**. One of the boxes
is tied to the arm, facing the heart. The
other is tied to the forehead. They remind
Jews to love God with their hearts and minds.

Jews fix a little oblong case to the doorpost at home. It has a tiny **scroll** inside, called a mezuzah, with a prayer written on it. Jewish people touch the mezuzah as they go in and out to remind them of God.

Friday night is the start of **Shabbat**, the Jewish day of rest and worship. At sunset, two candles are lit and a blessing is said to welcome in Shabbat.

Worshipping the Buddha

When Buddhists worship, they place offerings of flowers, candles and incense in front of the **Buddha**. They are reminded of the Buddha's life. He was an important teacher who taught people how to live kind and peaceful lives.

These are Buddhist **monks**. They wear special red or orange robes. They also shave their heads, give up their belongings and all their ties with the outside world to devote themselves to their beliefs.

Some Buddhists use prayer wheels as part of their worship. Inside the prayer wheels are scrolls with thousands of prayers on them. Some Buddhists spin prayer wheels to send the prayers flying out into the rest of the world.

This is a **bodhi tree**, a very special tree for Buddhists. The Buddha once sat under a tree like this to **meditate**. After many hours, hc understood the truth about life.

Christian Symbols

For Christians, the cross is a very special symbol. It reminds them of how Jesus Christ died on the cross and the belief that he rose from the dead to be with God.

Some Christians use a rosary to help them to say their prayers. A rosary is a necklace of beads with a cross hanging from it. As each bead is counted off, a prayer is spoken.

 At a service in church, the **altar** is laid out like a table with a large cup of wine and a plate containing **wafers** of bread. The priest or minister blesses the bread and wine.

The Christians sip a little wine and eat some bread in memory of Jesus. This reminds them of Jesus's last meal with his **disciples** before his death. This meal was called the Last Supper.

In some churches, Christians place candles next to a statue or picture of a **saint**. This is a statue of Mary, Jesus's mother, holding Jesus in her arms. As Christians light a candle, they say a prayer.

20

Muslim Prayers

Muslims say their prayers five times a day at fixed times. They can pray anywhere as long as it is clean. Some Muslims lay a prayer mat, like a small carpet, on the ground.

When Muslims pray, they must face towards the city of Makkah in Saudi Arabia. Here is the central **shrine** of Islam. There are special **compasses** to help them work out the direction of Makkah, wherever they are in the world.

This Muslim boy is using some prayer beads. As he counts off each bead, he says a prayer or recites one of the 99 names for **Allah**. Each string has 99 or 33 beads. The 33 beads are counted three times each.

Special to Sikhs

Sikhs have five special signs that show that they are Sikhs. These are called the five Ks. They are kesh (uncut hair), kangha (a wooden comb), kara (a steel bracelet), kirpan (a sword) and kachera (shorts).

Many Sikh men and older boys wear a turban to keep their long hair neat and tidy. Boys under the age of ten wear their hair in a top-knot covered with a piece of cloth called a patka.

A triangular yellow flag flies from all Sikh **gurdwaras**. It is called the Nishan Sahib, which means 'respected flag'. Its special symbol reminds Sikhs of their beliefs.

This beautiful cloth is called a **romalla**. It is used to cover the Guru Granth Sahib, the Sikh holy book. On the romalla is another Sikh symbol called the Ik Onkar which means 'There is only one God'.

Notes for teachers

Pages 4 & 5 The Hindu act of worship is called puja. It can take place in a mandir (temple) or at home. When Hindus visit the mandir, the worshippers bring flowers, fruit and sweets to offer to the deities. These offerings are called prashad. The priest takes them and offers them to the deities for their blessing. Then he returns them to the worshippers to bestow the gods' blessing on them. A tray of small lighted lamps may also be circled in front of the deity for his or her blessing.

Pages 6 & 7 Hindus do not only visit a mandir or shrine for puja but to have a darshana of the deity. This means a sight or viewing of the sacred images in the inner sanctum. These images are called murtis. Each mandir is dedicated to a god, goddess or holy person who represents God's presence on Earth, and whose murti stands in the inner sanctum. Hindus believe in thousands of deities who represent different aspects and characteristics of God whom they call Brahman, the Supreme Being. A priest sits near the murti in the inner sanctum of the temple. He is the only person who is allowed so close to the god or goddess. After he has taken offerings from worshippers, puja is performed and he marks the worshippers' foreheads with a tilak mark, a sign of blessing.

There are no set rules about where Hindus should worship. Most Hindu homes have an area set aside as a shrine. This may be a corner of a room, a single shelf or a whole puja room. At the end of the puja, lighted lamps may be circled in front of the deities while the worshippers sing a song of praise.

Pages 8 & 9 The tallit and tefillin are worn by Jewish men and boys over the age of 13. Boys often wear them for the first time at their Bar Mitzvah, the ceremony which marks their coming of age. The kippah is a small cap worn by men and boys. Some Jewish men wear it all the time. Others wear it only for services, as Jewish men must cover their heads to pray, as a mark of respect for God. The tallit is wrapped around the shoulders during prayer. It is normally white or cream, with black or blue stripes, and is made from wool, linen or silk. The fringes in the four corners, called tzizit, are reminders of the Ten Commandments. Tefillin, or phylacteries, are strapped to the forehead and arm for weekday prayers.

Pages 10 & 11 Every Jewish home should have a mezuzah fixed to the frame of most doors in the house.

It contains the handwritten words of the Shema prayer, the most important of the Jewish prayers.

The Jewish Shabbat lasts 25 hours, from sunset on Friday to sunset on Saturday. It is a very important day for Jews, not only as a holy day and a day of rest, but as a time for the family to enjoy being together. Shabbat begins on Friday evening when the wife or mother of the family lights two candles and says a blessing. If no woman is present, a man may light the candles. Shabbat ends on Saturday evening with the havdalah ceremony. Another special candle is lit, made of two thin candles plaited together to give several wicks to light. The father says prayers, then the candle is extinguished by dipping it in a saucer of wine. Shabbat is over.

Pages 12 & 13 Buddhists worship at viharas (temples or monasteries) and at shrines in their homes. Worship takes the form of paying respect to the Buddha, as symbolized by the Buddha in the shrine room. Buddhists do not worship the Buddha as a god but honour him as a great teacher and a remarkable human being. They are reminded of the Buddha's teachings and his special qualities of compassion, kindness and tranquillity. They are also reminded that they too can gain enlightenment, by following the Buddha's example. The offerings placed in front of the image have a special significance. Flowers look bright and fresh but eventually wilt and die, a reminder of the Buddha's teaching that nothing lasts for ever. The light from a candle removes the darkness in a room as the Buddha's teaching removes the darkness of ignorance. The sweet smell of incense is a reminder of the beauty of the Buddha's teaching.

These saffron-coloured robes are worn by monks when they are admitted to a monastery. The monks shave their heads to show that they have broken with all worldly ties and devoted their lives to the teachings of the Buddha. In some countries the robes worn by Buddhists may be maroon or black.

Pages 14 & 15 A prayer wheel is a cylinder containing a paper scroll with thousands of prayers on it. By spinning these wheels the prayers are released. Worshippers always walk around holy places clockwise, spinning the wheels with their right hands. This is because they believe that they should move around the Buddha the same way as the planets move around the Sun.

The bodhi tree is an extremely important symbol for Buddhists. The word 'bodhi' means wisdom or enlightenment. The Buddha was born a prince, Siddhartha Gautauma, who left behind a life of luxury to find the answer to life's suffering. While meditating under a fig tree in Bodh Gaya, India, he achieved enlightenment and understood the true meaning of life. He then became the Buddha, the enlightened one. The tree was renamed 'bodhi' after his achievement.

Pages 16 & 17 Because Jesus was crucified on a cross, the cross has become the most important Christian symbol. It reminds Christians of the sacrifice Jesus made on their behalf and of his Resurrection. The cross symbol can be seen in many places – inside churches, in the traditional shape of churches, and as rosaries, necklaces and badges. There are many different examples and designs.

Rosaries are strings of prayer beads used by Roman Catholics. The Rosary is actually the cycle of prayers said around the beads. These prayers are the main Christian prayers of the Lord's Prayer, the Hail Mary and the Glory. The creed is also said because it sums up the main Christian beliefs. The creed and prayers are recited on particular beads in a particular order.

Pages 18 &19 & 20 Holy Communion, at which worshippers share bread and wine, is the most important service in the Christian Church. It reminds Christians of Jesus's words to his disciples at the Last Supper telling them that this was his body and blood, about to be sacrificed for the sins of mankind. He commanded his followers to remember him by celebrating the supper. The Communion bread is placed on a plate called a paten. Ordinary bread is sometimes used but more usually there are special round wafers marked with a cross. The bread is consecrated as the 'body of Christ'. The cup or goblet which holds the wine is called the chalice. The wine is consecrated as the 'blood of Christ'.

The candles offered in churches are called votive candles. They are used in Roman Catholic and Orthodox churches, and in some Anglican churches.

Pages 21 & 22 & 23 Daily prayer is very important for Muslims. It is one of the Five Pillars of Islam, the five basic parts of Muslim life and belief. Muslims are required to perform ritual prayers (salah) five times a day, at dawn, midday, mid-afternoon, sunset and at night. This ensures that they remember Allah from early in the morning to last thing at night. They prepare for prayer by washing as the Qur'an prescribes (called wudu) and dressing decently. Prayers are said in Arabic and consist of praising God and reciting verses from the Qur'an. When they pray, Muslims must face towards the Ka'bah shrine in Makkah. This is the central shrine of Islam. Then they go through the set movements of prayer, called a rak'ah. They stand as they begin to pray, then bow, kneel and touch the ground. There are nine movements in a rak'ah. Muslims are not obliged to go to a mosque to pray, except for midday prayers on Friday, but the place they choose must be clean. In the mosque, a small arch called a mihrab indicates the direction of Makkah (the qiblah). Compasses can also be bought, with instruction books, to find the qiblah from major cities around the world.

Prayer beads are small, light beads that are either 33 beads divided into sections of 11, or 99 beads divided into sections of 33. It is said that a worshipper will earn his or her place in heaven by saying one of the 99 names of Allah for each of the prayer beads, as a form of worship.

Pages 24 & 25 The Five Ks are symbols of belonging to the Sikh faith. Their origins lie in the founding of the Khalsa, or Sikh 'brotherhood' by the tenth guru, Guru Gobind Singh which was established to protect and defend the Sikh faith, by force if necessary. They are known as the Five Ks because they all begin with the letter K in the Punjabi language. Kesh means not cutting hair or beards, in keeping with God's wishes. Kangha is a comb for keeping the hair tidy. Cleanliness and orderliness are important for Sikhs. Kara is a steel bracelet worn on the right wrist to symbolize strength and the unity of Sikhs with God. Kirpan is a sword which shows readiness to fight for truth. Kachera are shorts worn as underwear. These were more practical in battle than the usual baggy trousers or dhoti (traditional dress) worn in the Punjab. The Five Ks are worn by men and women alike because Sikhism stresses equality. Girls do not need to wear a turban, though some Sikh women do. For boys, a turban-tying ceremony is held when they are about ten years old. Before this, they wear their hair tied in a top-knot and covered with a handkerchief-sized piece of cloth called a patka.

Pages 26 & 27 The symbol on the Nishan Sahib flag is made of three parts. In the middle is a double-edged sword called a khanda. It is used during initiation ceremonies when Sikhs join the Khalsa, or Sikh community. The circle around it shows that God is one with no beginning or end. The two curved swords on either side represent spiritual and earthly power. Every spring, at the festival of Baisakhi, the Nishan Sahib is taken down and replaced. The Ik Onkar is another important Sikh symbol. It means 'There is only one God', the first line of the Mool Mantar, a hymn composed by Guru Nanak, the first Sikh guru.

Glossary

Allah The Muslim word for God.

altar A special table used in a Christian church.

bodhi tree The tree under which the Buddha sat to meditate. Its name means 'tree of wisdom'.

Buddha A great teacher who lived about 2,500 years ago. Buddhists follow his teachings as a guide through life.

compasses Instruments used for finding the direction of a place.

disciples Jesus's special followers and friends.

divas Small clay lamps used in Hindu worship.

gurdwaras Places where Sikhs go to worship.

Krishna A god who is known for his tricks and miracles.

mandir A place where Hindus go to worship. It is also called a temple.

meditate To think very hard and deeply about something.

monks Holy men who live very strict, simple lives.

romalla A cloth used for covering the Sikh holy book when it is not being used.

saint A very good and holy person.

scroll A rolled-up piece of paper.

Shabbat The Jewish day of rest and worship. It lasts from Friday night to Saturday night.

showing Standing for, or meaning.

shrine A place of worship either at home or in a holy building.

Torah The Jewish holy book.

wafers Thin circles of bread.

Books to read

HINDU
Diwali by Kerena Marchant (Wayland, 1996)

Hindu by Jenny Wood (Franklin Watts, 1996)

JEWISH
The Seventh Day is Shabbat by Margaret Barratt (Heinemann, 1994)

BUDDHIST
The Buddha's Birthday by Margaret Barratt (Heinemann, 1994)

My Buddhist Life by Meg St. Pierre and Marty Casey (Wayland, 1996)

CHRISTIAN
Prayers for Children by Christopher Herbert (The National Society, 1993)

Lucy's Sunday by Margaret Barratt (Heinemann, 1994)

Water into Wine by Alain Royer and Georges Carpentier (Heinemann, 1998)

SIKH
I am a Sikh by Manju Aggarwal (Watts, 1984)

My Sikh Life by Kanwaljit Kaur-Singh (Wayland, 1997)

GENERAL SERIES ON RELIGION:
Beliefs and Cultures series (Franklin Watts, 1997/8)
Everyday Religion series (Wayland, 1996/7)
Introducing Religions series (Heinemann, 1997)
Looking at Christianity series and **Looking at Judaism** series (Wayland, 1998)

Editor: Sarah Doughty
Design: Sterling Associates
Consultant: Alison Seaman

First published in 1998 by
Wayland Publishers Ltd
61 Western Road, Hove
East Sussex, BN3 1JD

© Copyright 1998 Wayland Publishers Ltd

Find Wayland on the Internet at http://www.wayland.co.uk

British Library Cataloguing in Publication Data
Ganeri, Anita
    Religious Articles. – (What's Special to me?)
    1. Religious articles – Juvenile literature
    I. Title
    291.3'7

ISBN 0 7502 2243 3

Printed and bound by G.Canale & C.S.p.A., Turin

Picture Acknowledgements: Bipinchandra J. Mistry 6; Circa Photo Library (Barrie Searle) title page, 5, 7, (Barrie Searle) 8, 10, (Barrie Searle) 10, 20 (left), (John Smith) 24; Getty Images (Nabeel Turner) 22; Sally and Richard Greenhill Photo Library (Richard Greenhill) 27; Robert Harding 9, 12, 15; Christine Osborne Pictures 4, 17, 18, 21, 25 (left and right), 26; Peter Sanders 23; Trip (T Bognar) 13, (B Vikander) 14, (H Rogers) 16; Wayland Picture Library (Jenny Woodcock) cover, 3, (Jenny Woodcock) 19; Zefa 11, 20 (right).

Index